Baby tips
for mums

Simon Brett

Bestselling author of *How to be a Little Sod*

summersdale

Baby Tips for Mums

Copyright © Simon Brett, 2005

Reprinted 2005, 2006 and 2007

The right of Simon Brett to be identified as the author of this work has been asserted in accordance with sections 77 and 78 of the Copyright, Designs and Patents Act 1988.

Summersdale Publishers Ltd
46 West Street
Chichester
West Sussex
PO19 1RP
UK

www.summersdale.com

Printed and bound by Tien Wah Press, Singapore

ISBN: 1 84024 528 X
ISBN 13: 978 1 84024 528 8

Contents

Introduction

Well, there you are. You've put in all that hard work. You've spent nine months producing what is undoubtedly the most beautiful and intelligent baby in the world, and you'd have thought the one thing you really deserve now is a nice long rest. The trouble is, that's not the way the baby sees things. Nor frequently is it the way your partner or other family members will see things. So, to help you survive what is going to be an unfairly busy stage of your life, here are a few tips…

5

Mum's the Word

Basic Rules:

In the early weeks a New Mum must prepare herself for a lot of screaming and tantrums – and that's just from her partner.

The relationship between a New Mum and her Baby is a power struggle… and you may as well face the fact straight away – the Baby's going to win.

When breastfeeding, don't think of yourself as a canteen. Thinking of yourself as a gourmet restaurant is much better for your self-esteem.

Basic Rules:

With Babies, everything
ends in tears... from
one or other of you.

Getting your figure back after you've had your Baby is an admirable ambition, but then so is world peace... and finding an NHS dentist... and pigs flying...

When a Baby is being dressed, either it seems to develop one more limb or the garment seems to develop one less hole.

The night after you said your Baby slept through the night for the first time, it won't.

For the convenience
of Parents, Baby
Buggies fold. For the
inconvenience of Parents,
Babies don't.

You must never say that your Baby is prettier/ better-natured/more intelligent than anyone else's... even though it's obviously true.

However much you would like it to be, a Baby will never be a matching accessory.

You can always
recognise a New
Mum by:

The deep hollows
under her eyes.

You can always recognise a New Mum by:

The encrustation of puke
over her shoulder.

You can always recognise a New Mum by:

The fact that she's still in her dressing gown at lunchtime.

You can always recognise a New Mum by:

The lingering aroma
of sterilising fluid.

You can always recognise a New Mum by:

Her inability to sustain
adult conversation.

You can always recognise a New Mum by:

The disappointed,
neglected look in her
partner's eyes.

Daddy
Dearest

You can tell your partner will be a good Dad when:

He offers to look after the Baby while you go off for a girlie weekend with your friends. (Oh yes?)

He says, 'The Baby
was crying in the
night, but you looked
so peacefully asleep
that I sorted everything
out.' (Come on!)

He's decided that, now
he's got the responsibility
of a Baby, he's going to
give up drinking with
the boys and stay at
home every evening.
(Let's get back to the
real world, shall we?)

Your partner should be discouraged from:

Getting into
discussions with
your mother about

A) Childcare,
B) Education,
C) Anything, really...

Your partner should be discouraged from:

Wanting to dress your Baby in any team strip.

Your partner should be discouraged from:

Asking if he can take his paternity leave in cash and keep working.

Pretending, when you're breast-feeding in public, that he's with someone else.

Your partner should be discouraged from:

Thinking that 'wetting the Baby's head' should continue on a nightly basis until after it's finished school.

Mummy Training

For a Baby it's a point of honour to:

Come up with an illness
which doesn't match
any of the descriptions
in the childcare books.

For a Baby it's a point of honour to:

Hold back a really big Poo until immediately after a nappy change.

For a Baby it's a point of honour to:

Listen out for the words, 'I think the Baby's settled for the night now,' and prove them wrong.

For a Baby it's a point of honour to:

Know when its Mum
really wants to show it off
and develop a nasty facial
rash just before the event.

Be prepared for
your mother to say
the following:

'You think your labour
was tough, but let me tell
you, when I had you...'

'I love your Baby very much, but I don't want to be thought of as a free babysitting service.'

Be prepared for your mother
to say the following:

'Just because you've had
a Baby, that's no excuse
to let yourself go.'

'Everybody says I
look far too young to
be a grandmother.'

The New
Mum's
Dictionary

ANAEMIA : This fashion for giving Babies Victorian names is really getting out of hand.

The New Mum's Dictionary:

AU PAIR : A young woman whose presence in the house gives you time to yourself, and your partner ideas.

BABYSITTING CIRCLE : A reciprocal arrangement whereby Parents seem to spend every night looking after other people's children and then find nobody's free on the one evening *they* want to go out.

BABY WALKER : A father at 3 a.m., having been told that 'a few turns round the block may make the Baby settle'.

BATHTIME : A daily contest between Baby and Parent to see who can get wetter, invariably – though unwillingly – won by the Parent.

BEDTIME STORY : A childish fantasy – like, for instance, the idea that your Baby goes to bed and to sleep at the same time every night.

BREAST PADS :
Equipment used
by women cricketers.

BURPING : Something you have to do for your Baby, but which your partner can manage without any help from anyone.

COMFORTER : Whatever works for you (partner, lover, Celine Dion CD, big box of chocolates, Maeve Binchy novel, Chardonnay, gin, etc.)

CONTRACEPTION, MOST EFFECTIVE METHOD AFTER BABY'S BIRTH : The Baby.

FEEDING TRAY : An attachment to a High Chair, something for a Baby to push food off.

The New Mum's Dictionary:

HEARING TEST : The moment at the doctor's when your Baby, who up until that point has been woken by the sound of a fly landing on a cushion in another room, is suddenly unable to hear a drum being banged next to its ear.

INTRODUCTION OF SOLIDS : The Baby's discovery that Lego bricks fit into its mouth.

LABOUR : The process of giving birth, so called because it's BLOODY HARD WORK.

(cf. NEW LABOUR : The idea that, along with everything else, having a Baby will become pain-free. Or any other unfulfilled promise.)

The New Mum's Dictionary:

LOOSE STOOLS : The curse of IKEA strikes again.

NAPPY RASH : All-purpose explanation for any bad behaviour from Baby.

OTHER MUMS : Most
probably, your salvation.
There'll always be one
who's worse at the whole
business than you are.

The New Mum's Dictionary:

PARENTAL DISCIPLINE:
When there's a New
Baby in the house, it is
important to establish
who's boss. But don't
worry about it. Most
Parents come into
line pretty quickly.

PROJECTILE VOMITING :
Shooting from the lip.

ROLE MODEL : Someone who has completely got her figure back after having a Baby.

The New Mum's Dictionary:

ROLL MODEL :

A) What you look like, having completely failed to get your figure back after having a Baby.

B) The little figurine of a ROLE MODEL you make out of bread, to stick pins in.

STERILISATION :
Procedure recommended
for dirty nappies and
dirty-minded partners.

TEETHING : All-purpose explanation for any bad behaviour from baby.

TEETHING RING : A group of Babies who all decide to whinge at the same time.

WEANING : Getting your Baby off the breast. Any Baby worth its salt can make this process last for years.

WIND : All-purpose explanation for any bad behaviour from Baby.

A FINAL
THOUGHT...

When your Baby's being
a right little pain, and you
see a sign reading 'Baby
Changing Facilities'...
don't even think about it.

Baby tips
for grandparents

Simon Brett
Bestselling author of *How to be a Little Sod*

Baby tips
for dads

Simon Brett
Bestselling author of *How to be a Little Sod*

Whether you are a rookie dad or the seasoned grandparent of a lively horde, make these little books the latest additions to your household.

www.summersdale.com